Essential Number Skills

Activity Book

Written by
Norman D Lock

Illustrated by
Andrew Warrington

Contents

- Multiplication 2
- Division 7
- Fractions 12
- Decimals 17
- Percentages 22

- in your head
- on paper
- with decimals

Multiplication

A quicker way of adding 2 + 2 + 2 + 2 + 2 + 2 is to say **6 lots of 2** (6 × 2). Or we could say **2 lots of 6** (2 × 6). The answer is still 12. Saying **2 lots of 6** or **2 times 6** or **2 × 6** is called multiplying.

In multiplying, the order of the numbers doesn't matter, however many there are.

2 × 3 × 5 = 30
3 × 5 × 2 = 30

Multiplying in your head

To be able to multiply quickly on paper or in your head it helps to learn multiplication facts (times tables) off by heart.

To multiply a number by **10**, move it **one place to the left** and fill the space on the right with a zero. To multiply it by **100**, move it **two places to the left** and fill in to the right with **two** zeros.

1 Use all your mental arithmetic skills to answer these questions as quickly as possible. Write your answers in the boxes.

a 3 × 70 = 210
b 90 × 5 = 450
c 4 × 19 = 360
d 59 × 6 = 336
e 3 × 400 = 1200
f 500 × 7 = 3500
g 20 × 90 =
h 3 × 68 =

2 For each flight, the space shuttle needs the following supplies. In your head, work out what would be needed for 10 flights.

a 14 snack trolleys [ ]

b 567 space shades [ ]

c 123 fuel modules [ ]

3 After each flight, the space shuttle unloads these items. What would the total number of items unloaded after 100 flights be?

a 23 litter bags [ ]

b 150 supply boxes [ ]

c 500 lost items [ ]

4 The shuttle carries souvenirs from the planet Multo. In your head, work out the total values in pounds and pence.

a 10 pencils at 17p each £ [ ]

b 100 Multo-chews at 5p each £ [ ]

c 10 Mount Urg snow domes at £4·05 each £ [ ]

5 Arco Tekt is designing a shuttle for a planet with very big inhabitants! Do his calculations in your head and fill in the answers.

a A 25mm light switch 10 times larger [ ] mm or [ ] cm

b A 1·375m space toilet 100 times larger [ ] m

6 On long journeys, the hovering computer sets puzzles. Use your knowledge of times tables facts to fill in the missing numbers.

a

×	2	5	
3		18	
		24	
7	35		63
	40		

b

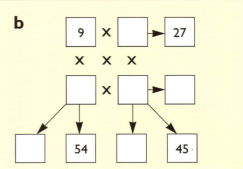

Multiplying on paper

Captain Aag, there are 4 space hoppers approaching, each with 235 passengers on board.

How many passengers is that altogether?

To find the answer, multiply 235 by 4.

Start with the units column.
4 times 5 units is 20 (2 tens).
Put a 0 in the units column and carry the 2 to the tens column.

```
H T U
2 3 5
    4 ×
    0
  2
```

4 times 3 tens is 12 tens (120).
12 tens plus the 2 tens carried over is 14 tens (140).
Put the 4 in the tens column and carry the 1 hundred to the hundreds column.

```
H T U
2 3 5
    4 ×
  4 0
1 2
```

4 times 2 hundreds is 8 hundreds (800).
8 hundreds plus the 1 hundred carried over is 9 hundreds (900).
Write 9 in the hundreds column.

```
H T U
2 3 5
    4 ×
9 4 0
1 2
```

There are 940 passengers altogether.

7 On a separate piece of paper, work out these problems and write the answers in the white boxes.

a The space shuttle travels to the Planet Multo 157 times every Earth week. How many times does it visit the planet in 3 weeks?

b Multoan spacecraft each have 148 windows. How many windows are there on 4 spacecraft?

c Multoans have 6 fingers on each hand. How many fingers do 623 Multoans have?

Multiplication times

When you have a problem to solve, look out for key words that tell you what kind of calculation to do. If you see phrases like these, the calculation will be a **multiplication**.

3 lots of £4.00

3 sets of 6 books

6 times 7

the **multiples** of 9

7 groups of 4 spacecraft

THE PRODUCT OF 4 and 5

How much do I need for 3 tickets?

Multiplying decimal numbers is simple.

Tickets to Multo are 3.25 Earth pounds each.

3 times 5 pence is 15p.
Put the 5p in the pence column and carry 1 ten pence (10p) into the ten-pence column.

£	Ten pence	Pence
3 .	2	5
		3 ×
		5
	1	

3 times 2 ten-pence coins (3 × 20p) is 6 ten-pence coins (60p).
Add the 1 ten-pence coin (10p) carried over to make 7 ten-pence coins (70p).
Write 7 in the ten-pence column.

£	Ten pence	Pence
3 .	2	5
		3 ×
	7	5
	1	

3 times £3 is £9.
Put 9 in the £ (pounds) column.

£	Ten pence	Pence
3 .	2	5
		3 ×
9 .	7	5
	1	

3 tickets to Multo cost £9·75 altogether.

How much do 7 postcards of Multo cost if they are 46p each?

Putting in the decimal point helps to keep all the numbers in the right columns.

£	Ten pence	Pence
0 .	4	6
		7 ×
3 .	2	2
3	4	

8 On a separate piece of paper, work out the cost of buying these items from the space terminal shop for a group holidaying on Multo. Write the totals in the spaces.

a 6 badges £

b 5 guide books £

c 10 boxes of tablets £

d 6 Multoan phrase books £

e 100 guide books £

Guide books £3.75 each

Badges 27p each

Multoan phrase book £1.72 each

Space sickness tablets £4.95 for a box

To multiply by a number of more than 1 digit, first multiply by the units digit and write the answer underneath as usual. Then move to the tens column and write the answer on the next line down. Put a 0 in the units column as you are multiplying by 10. Finally, add the two answers together.

```
 Th   H   T   U
      4   7   1
          1   2  ×
      9   4   2    (2 × 471)
 +4   7   1   0    (10 × 471)
  5   6   5   2
```

Multo sweets come in tins of 471. How many in 12 tins?

9 Now use all your multiplication skills to find the answers to these problems. Use a separate piece of paper to work out those that you cannot do in your head, and write the answers in the boxes.

a How many days are there in 9 Earth weeks?

b What is the cost of 100 labels at 25p each?

c What is the product of 3, 4 and 5?

d The landing lights on Multo have been set out in rows of 26. How many lights in 8 rows?

e What is the cost of 127 metres of fuel piping at 80p per metre?

f Each shuttle fuel tank holds 53 litres. How many litres would all 12 tanks hold when full?

- short method
- long method
- short cuts

Division

There are 745 checks to be made before take-off and 5 crew to share the work equally.

How many checks does each crew member make?

To find the answer, we need to **divide** 745 by 5.

$$745 \div 5$$
$$\frac{745}{5}$$
$$5\overline{)745}$$

These are all ways of writing down **745 divided by 5**.

Dividing on paper

To work out 745 ÷ 5, we can use the **short division method**.

5 into 7 goes once with 2 over. Put 1 above the 7 and carry the 2 into the next column.

$$\begin{array}{r} 1 \\ 5\overline{)7^{2}45} \end{array}$$

5 into 24 goes 4 times with 4 over. Write 4 above the ²4 and carry the 4 left over into the next column.

$$\begin{array}{r} 1\,4 \\ 5\overline{)7^{2}4^{4}5} \end{array}$$

5 into 45 goes 9 exactly. There is nothing left over and no more numbers to divide.

$$\begin{array}{r} 1\,4\,9 \\ 5\overline{)7^{2}4^{4}5} \end{array}$$

If 745 pre-flight checks are shared equally by 5 crew, each crew member does 149 checks.

Look out for zero...

Look at this short division.
3 into 1 does not go. We don't begin numbers with a zero, so leave a space above the 1 and carry that 1 into the next column.
3 into 15 goes 5 with no remainder.
Write a 5 above the ¹5 and move on to the next column.
3 into 2 does not go. **Write a zero above the 2** and carry the 2 into the next column.
3 into 21 goes 7 with no remainder. Write 7 above the ²1.
Apart from the first column, each column must have a digit in the answer space. Write a zero if there is no answer for a column.

$$\begin{array}{r} 507 \\ 3\overline{)1^{1}52^{2}1} \end{array}$$

The planet Multo has poisonous slugs, which are luckily very rare.

The shuttle is carrying 4212 capsules of antidote in 12 boxes.

How many capsules are there in each box, if all 12 contain the same number?

To find the answer, we need to divide 4212 by 12.
We can use the **long division method**.

12 into 4 does not go. Move on to the next column.
12 into 42 goes 3 times.
Write 3 above the 2 at the top.

3 times 12 (3 × 12) = 36. Write 36 under the 42 and take it away to find the remainder, which is 6.

Bring down the next digit (1) next to the 6.
The arrow shows how. 12 into 61 goes 5 times.
Write the 5 at the top above the 1.

5 times 12 (5 × 12) = 60. Write 60 under the 61 and take it away to find the remainder, which is 1.

Bring down the next digit (2) next to the 1.
The arrow shows how. 12 into 12 goes once exactly.
Write 1 at the top. Write 12 under the 12 and take away.

There is no remainder and no more numbers to divide.
The answer is written at the top.

```
         351
     12)4212
       - 36↓
          61
        - 60↓
           12
         - 12
           00
```

4212 divided by 12 = 351

There are 351 capsules in each box.

1 Write the answers to these problems in the spaces. Do your working out on a separate piece of paper.

a 105 flights are shared equally between 3 space shuttles. How many flights does each make? ☐

b There are 568 passengers on the next flight. If 4 crew members share their care equally, how many passengers does each look after? ☐

c The 2442 planets in the galaxy are divided into 6 equal sectors. How many in each sector? ☐

d If 9128 space stamps are shared equally by 7 collectors, how many does each have? ☐

2 Complete these division chains by dividing each number in turn by the number at the beginning. Use a separate piece of paper for your working out.

a ÷ 2   256 — 128 — ☐ — ☐ — ☐ — 8 — ☐

b ÷ 5   625 — ☐ — ☐ — ☐ — ☐

c ÷ 4   ☐ — 192 — ☐ — ☐ — ☐

d ÷ 7   4802 — 686 — ☐ — ☐ — 2

3 Use long division to solve these problems. Use a separate piece of paper for your working out and write your final answers in the boxes.

a There are 2832 packs of space rations on the shuttle. They are packed in boxes of 12. How many boxes of 12 are there altogether? ☐

b 4815 ÷ 15 = ☐

c $\frac{6075}{25}$ = ☐

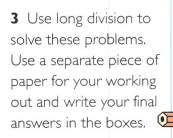

Division data...

If these key words appear in a problem, they are signs that you need to do a division calculation to find the answer.

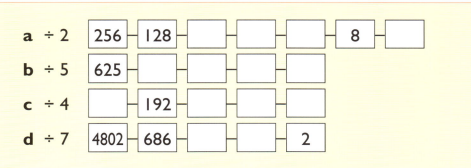

- **divide** by 6
- **divide equally** into 8 parts
- **share** out into 7 equal parts
- **how many 9s in** 54?
- **how many lots of** 4 are there in 32?
- **how many times will 5 go into** 40?

4 Follow the hovering computer's instructions, doing your working out on a separate piece of paper.

Think of a 3-digit number and write it here:

Now write the same 3 digits again immediately after it to make a 6-digit number:

Divide the 6-digit number by 7 =

Divide the answer by 11 =

Divide your last answer by 13 =

What number are you left with?

Try it with other 3-digit numbers. Does it always work?

To make the trick work with 2-digit numbers, put a zero before writing the number again to make a 5 digit number. (For example, 35 becomes 35035.)

Sometimes you can avoid doing a long division by cutting the numbers in half. As long as you halve **both numbers** in the division, the answer will stay the same. Keep halving until one of the numbers becomes an odd number (ending in 1, 3, 5, 7 or 9).

$24\overline{)600}$ Half of 24 is 12. Half of 600 is 300.

$12\overline{)300}$ Half of 12 is 6. Half of 300 is 150.

$6\overline{)150}$ Half of 6 is 3. Half of 150 is 75.

$3\overline{)7^15}$ 25

The answer is 25. Check that this works by using your calculator to work out 600 ÷ 24. Without a calculator, it is easier to divide by 3 than by 24.

5 On a separate piece of paper, make these divisions easier by halving. Write the final answers in the boxes.

a $14\overline{)644}$ =

b $12\overline{)2820}$ =

c $36\overline{)864}$ =

d $16\overline{)512}$ =

This rule is not just true for halving. In division, you can do anything to numbers to make them easier to work out (for instance, double them, or divide them by 5, 10, or 100) **as long as you do the same to both numbers**.

6 Treat both of the numbers in these divisions in the same way to make them easier. Use a separate piece of paper for your working if you need to.

a 5)325 =

b 560 ÷ 70 =

c $\frac{3600}{600}$ =

d 5)435 =

e 90)1260 =

f 27,200 ÷ 800 =

7 Use all your division skills to find the answers to these questions. Do any working out on a separate piece of paper and write the answers in the boxes.

a 91 days   How many weeks?

b 270 toes   How many humans?

c 162 sides   How many triangles?

d 288 faces   How many cubes?

e 1296 legs   How many cows?

f 2024 legs   How many octopuses?

g What is the nearest number to 320 that can be divided exactly by 7? (There should be no remainder.)

h How many 25p space stamps can I buy for £25?

i 400 spacesuits have been delivered in anti-gravity boxes. Each box holds 8 spacesuits. How many boxes are there?

j If power fails at the space terminal, 180 emergency lights are used. They are put in 12 equal rows. How many lights in each row?

- equal parts
- improper
- equivalent

Fractions

Fractions are numbers that are **less than one unit** or **less than one whole**.

The number at the top of a fraction is called the **numerator**.

The number at the bottom of a fraction is called the **denominator**.

The **denominator** shows how many **equal parts** something is divided into.
The **numerator** shows how many of these **equal parts** we are thinking about.

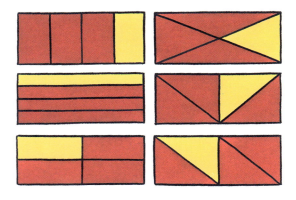

Each space shuttle in the Multoan fleet has a rectangular badge which is $\frac{1}{4}$ yellow and $\frac{3}{4}$ red. $\frac{1}{4}$ and $\frac{3}{4}$ are fractions of the whole badge.

The badge is divided into 4 equal parts, one of which is painted yellow and three of which are painted red.

The badges of all the shuttles are different but they are all $\frac{1}{4}$ yellow and $\frac{3}{4}$ red.

1 Badges of shuttles from other fleets are different shapes with different fractions coloured. Next to each badge, write the fraction of the badge that is coloured red.

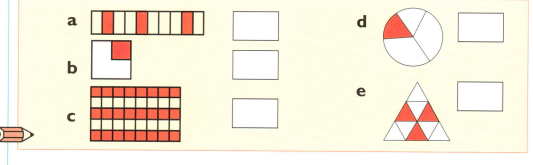

2 Colour in these badges so that each one is $\frac{1}{2}$ white and $\frac{1}{2}$ red but no two badges are the same.

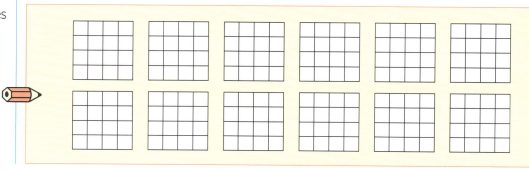

There are 36 Multoan passengers this morning. $\frac{3}{4}$ of them are wearing hats.

How many are wearing hats?

To find the answer, draw a box and divide it into 4 equal parts. Each part is $\frac{1}{4}$. The box represents 36 passengers. To divide them into quarters, we have to divide 36 equally between the 4 parts. That means there are 9 in each part. **Three** quarters ($\frac{3}{4}$) will be **3** of those parts.

There are 27 hat-wearing Multoans!

$\frac{1}{4}$ of 36 = 9
In other words: 36 ÷ 4 = 9

$\frac{3}{4}$ of 36 = 3 × 9 = 27

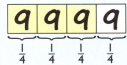

3 Draw boxes on a separate piece of paper to solve these problems. Write the answers in the boxes here.

a 30 passengers are having a drink. $\frac{1}{6}$ of them have chosen yarg juice. How many is that?

b 56 Multoans are watching the film. $\frac{3}{8}$ of them have seen it before. How many have **not** seen it?

Drawing boxes can help to solve other problems too.

A shuttle-spotter's notebook please! Here's 80p.

*How much **does** it cost?*

That's only $\frac{2}{3}$ of the cost!

Draw a box to represent the whole cost of the notebook and divide it into 3 equal parts.

The whole cost of the notebook is £1·20.

2 of the parts ($\frac{2}{3}$) hold a total of 80p. That means that each of the 2 parts has 40p. The third part (the remaining $\frac{1}{3}$) must also contain 40p because all the parts are equal.

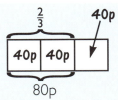

That means that the whole box contains 3 × 40p = 120p = £1·20

4 Draw shapes on a separate piece of paper to help find the answer to these problems.

  a $\frac{1}{2}$ costs £3.50. The whole costs ☐

  b $\frac{1}{3}$ is 70p. The whole thing is ☐

  c $\frac{2}{3}$ of Zed's money is £1. How much is all of it? ☐

Improper fractions

I've painted $\frac{10}{3}$.

*How many is **that**?*

Fractions that are top-heavy, where the numerator is bigger than the denominator, are called **improper fractions**.

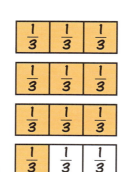

Look at Vork's painting. Ten thirds ($\frac{10}{3}$) is the same as saying 3 whole ones and 1 third. It is written $3\frac{1}{3}$. We can work this out without seeing Vork's work:

$\frac{10}{3}$ means 10 divided by 3 (10 ÷ 3).
10 ÷ 3 = 3 with $\frac{1}{3}$ left over. So $\frac{10}{3} = 3\frac{1}{3}$.

Here are some more examples: $\frac{5}{4} = 1\frac{1}{4}$ $\frac{7}{5} = 1\frac{2}{5}$ $\frac{6}{2} = 3$

5 Write these improper fractions as whole numbers and fractions.

  a $\frac{7}{4}$ = ☐   **c** $\frac{16}{4}$ = ☐

  b $\frac{5}{3}$ = ☐   **d** $\frac{25}{2}$ = ☐

Equivalent fractions

How much have you checked today?

Wyz, Xil, Yot and Zed are checking stores. Each large storage bay contains boxes of different sizes.

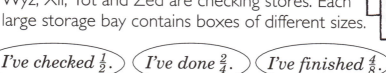

I've checked $\frac{1}{2}$.   *I've done $\frac{2}{4}$.*   *I've finished $\frac{4}{8}$.*   *Err... $\frac{8}{16}$.*

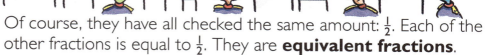

Of course, they have all checked the same amount: $\frac{1}{2}$. Each of the other fractions is equal to $\frac{1}{2}$. They are **equivalent fractions**.

Making equivalent fractions

If any number is multiplied by 1, the answer is the same number.

$12 \times 1 = 12$

The number 1 can be written as a fraction.

$1 = \frac{2}{2} = \frac{3}{3} = \frac{4}{4} = \frac{5}{5}$ and so on.

Multiplying a number by these fractions is the same as multiplying it by 1. To make an equivalent fraction for $\frac{1}{3}$, multiply $\frac{1}{3}$ by 1 written as a fraction.

$\frac{1}{3} \times \frac{2}{2}$

To multiply fractions, first multiply the top numbers (the numerators) together: and then multiply the bottom numbers together:

$\frac{1 \times 2 = 2}{3 \times 2 = 6}$

$\frac{1}{3} \times \frac{2}{2} = \frac{2}{6}$ So $\frac{1}{3}$ is equal to $\frac{2}{6}$

By multiplying $\frac{1}{3}$ by 1 written as different fractions, we can make more equivalent fractions.

$\frac{1}{3} \times \frac{3}{3} = \frac{3}{9}$ $\frac{1}{3} \times \frac{4}{4} = \frac{4}{12}$ and so on.

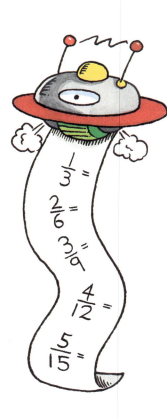

6 Use this method to fill in the missing numbers and complete these lists of equivalent fractions.

a $\frac{1}{2} = \frac{5}{10} = \frac{3}{6} = \frac{\square}{8} = \frac{6}{\square} = \frac{\square}{18} = \frac{10}{\square}$

b $\frac{2}{3} = \frac{4}{6} = \frac{6}{\square} = \frac{\square}{12} = \frac{10}{\square} = \frac{\square}{18} = \frac{16}{24}$

I've stacked $\frac{3}{5}$ of my boxes.

I've piled up $\frac{2}{3}$ of mine.

Comparing fractions

These fractions can be compared by changing them into equivalent fractions.

$\frac{3}{5}$ $\frac{2}{3}$

Look at the denominators:

$\frac{3}{5} \times \frac{3}{3} = \frac{9}{15}$ $\frac{2}{3} \times \frac{5}{5} = \frac{10}{15}$

5 and 3 can both be multiplied to make 15. Both the fractions can be changed to 15ths like this:

$\frac{3}{5}$ is equal to $\frac{9}{15}$ $\frac{2}{3}$ is equal to $\frac{10}{15}$

So $\frac{2}{3}$ is greater. $\frac{2}{3} > \frac{3}{5}$

7 Work out if the fractions in each pair are equivalent or not. Put the correct sign between them.

a $\frac{1}{2}$ ☐ $\frac{3}{8}$ c $\frac{1}{4}$ ☐ $\frac{1}{5}$ e $\frac{2}{5}$ ☐ $\frac{1}{3}$

b $\frac{1}{3}$ ☐ $\frac{4}{12}$ d $\frac{2}{3}$ ☐ $\frac{3}{4}$ f $\frac{5}{6}$ ☐ $\frac{7}{8}$

> is greater than
< is less than
= is equal to

$\frac{15}{20}$ of the passengers are on board, Captain.

*What on Multo does **that** mean?*

Cancelling down

Cancelling down means reducing a fraction to its simplest form. It means finding the simplest equivalent fraction.

This time, instead of multiplying by 1, **divide** by 1. Find the biggest number you can that divides into both the denominator and the numerator, into both 15 and 20. That number is 5. Dividing by $\frac{5}{5}$ is the same as dividing by 1.

$\frac{15}{20} \div \frac{5}{5} = \frac{15 \div 5}{20 \div 5} = \frac{3}{4}$

$\frac{3}{4}$ is the simplest form of $\frac{15}{20}$

8 Cancel down these fractions. Do your working out on another piece of paper if necessary.

a $\frac{6}{12}$ = ☐   c $\frac{8}{12}$ = ☐   e $\frac{12}{15}$ = ☐

b $\frac{5}{15}$ = ☐   d $\frac{15}{18}$ = ☐   f $\frac{18}{24}$ = ☐

Cancelling down fractions can help us solve problems.

9 Use all your skills in dealing with fractions to answer these questions. Work them out on a separate piece of paper and write the answers in the boxes.

a There were 12 crew in the galley. 9 of them were eating. What fraction was eating? ☐

b In a crew of 150 Multoans and humans, $\frac{2}{5}$ were humans. How many were Multoans? ☐

c The crew do first aid drill for $\frac{1}{4}$ hour each day. How long do they practise in one Earth week? ☐

d In its last 144 flights, the shuttle was on time for $\frac{5}{8}$ of the flights and late for $\frac{1}{6}$ of them. For the rest of the flights, it was early! How many times was that? ☐

- decimal digits
- decimals to fractions
- using decimals

Decimals

Decimals, like fractions, are numbers that are **smaller than one unit**. Decimal numbers are written on the right of the decimal point. The **decimal point** separates whole numbers from decimal fractions.

H   T   U   • $\frac{1}{10}$ $\frac{1}{100}$ $\frac{1}{1000}$

Getting bigger ← whole numbers | parts of whole numbers (decimal fractions) → Getting smaller

In our number system of **place value**, a number gets ten times smaller if it moves to the next column to the right. A **ten** is ten times smaller than a **hundred**. A **unit** is ten times smaller than a **ten**. This keeps on happening **after** the decimal point.

1 unit   decimal point $\frac{1}{10}$ $\frac{1}{100}$ $\frac{1}{1000}$

1 Write as a decimal how much of these 1-unit squares is shaded and unshaded. Remember that the total each time should be one whole one (1 or 1·0 or 1·00).

a Shaded: ☐   b Shaded: ☐   c Shaded: ☐
  Unshaded: ☐   Unshaded: ☐   Unshaded: ☐
  Total: ☐   Total: ☐   Total: ☐

Decimals are used to write down amounts of money.

£1·11
1 whole pound $\frac{1}{10}$ of £1 = 10p $\frac{1}{100}$ of £1 = 1p

Decimals are used to write down measurements.

1·111m
1 whole metre
$\frac{1}{10}$ of 1 metre = 10cm
$\frac{1}{100}$ of 1 metre = 1cm
$\frac{1}{1000}$ of 1 metre = 1mm

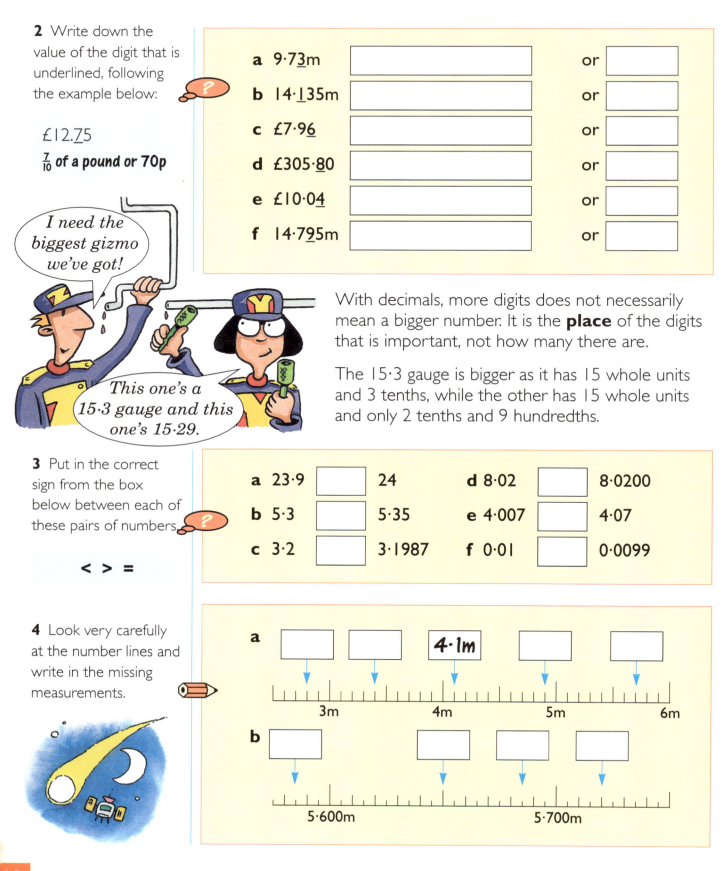

Changing decimals into fractions

It is easy to change **decimals** into **ordinary fractions** if you remember what each decimal is worth.

$$0.3 = \frac{3}{10} \qquad 0.04 = \frac{4}{100} \qquad 0.59 = \frac{59}{100}$$
$$0.006 = \frac{6}{1000} \qquad 0.014 = \frac{14}{1000}$$

What is 0·2 as a fraction?

Sometimes the fractions need to be cancelled down.

0·2 is the same as $\frac{2}{10}$.

To cancel down $\frac{2}{10}$, find the largest number that can be divided into both the numerator and the denominator (into 2 and 10). The largest number is 2.

$$\frac{2}{10} \div \frac{2}{2} = \frac{2 \div 2}{10 \div 2} = \frac{1}{5}$$

0·2 as a fraction is $\frac{1}{5}$

5 Change these decimals into fractions, cancelling down if possible. Use a separate piece of paper for your working if necessary.

a 0·5 =

b 0·8 =

c 0·15 =

d 1·6 =

e 4·25 =

f 3·05 =

g 6·75 =

h 5·35 =

Zero point...

Remember that any whole number can be written with as many zeros as you like **after the decimal point** to help with a calculation. 1 is the same as 1·0 and 1·00 and 1·000000000! This means that you can keep dividing to deal with any remainders.

I'M 1·00000000000 IN A MILLION!

Changing fractions into decimals is easy too.

$\frac{1}{5}$ means 1 divided by 5. To change a fraction into a decimal **divide the numerator by the denominator**. In this case, divide 1 by 5.

That is easy with a calculator but it can be done on paper too. Notice that 1 is written as 1·00.

1 divided by 5 is not possible. Put a zero at the top.
We do this to draw attention to the decimal point.
Carry the 1 over into the tenths column.
We have passed the decimal point, so we put a decimal point at the top next to the first zero.
10 tenths divided by 5 is 2 tenths.
Put a 2 at the top in the tenths column.
There is nothing more to divide.

$$\begin{array}{r} 0\cdot 2 \\ 5\overline{\smash{)}1\cdot{}^10\,0} \end{array}$$

$\frac{1}{5} = 0\cdot 2$

Just as with any calculation, it is important to keep the digits properly lined up and to keep the decimal point in the correct place.

Sometimes you can change a fraction into a decimal in your head.

The first digit after the decimal point stands for tenths, so $\frac{3}{10}$ is 0·3.

6 Change these fractions into decimals. Do as many as you can in your head and use a separate piece of paper to work out the rest.

a $\frac{1}{2}$ =

b $\frac{1}{4}$ =

c $\frac{1}{8}$ =

d $\frac{4}{5}$ =

e $\frac{7}{10}$ =

f $\frac{9}{1000}$ =

7 Here are the take-off times, in seconds, for the shuttle's last 8 trips. List them in order, starting with the fastest.

10·02   9·98   10·20   10·00   9·99   9·89   10·15   10·12

8 The shuttle's Transformer machine takes in decimal numbers, splits up the digits and sends them out as fractions. The example above shows how it **should** work. Complete the others while the machine is mended. Don't forget to cancel down.

$1 \cdot 31 = \quad 1 + \frac{3}{10} + \frac{1}{100} \quad$ or $\quad 1\frac{31}{100}$

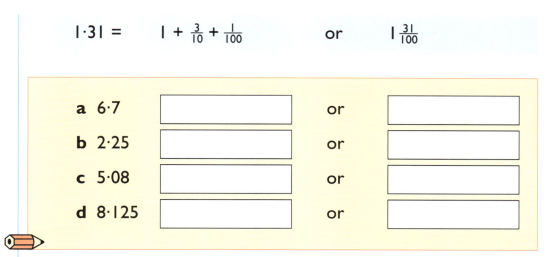

a 6·7 ⬚ or ⬚
b 2·25 ⬚ or ⬚
c 5·08 ⬚ or ⬚
d 8·125 ⬚ or ⬚

9 Each of the shuttle's space hoppers has a trip meter to show how far it has travelled. The digit on the red background equals one tenth ($\frac{1}{10}$) of a mile. The meters are shown at the beginning of the journeys. Fill in what they will show after journeys **a**, **b**, **c** and **d**.

Hopper 1: H T U · $\frac{1}{10}$ — 0 7 5 8
Hopper 2: H T U · $\frac{1}{10}$ — 3 4 0 9

a After $\frac{1}{10}$ mile
b After 1 mile
c After $1\frac{1}{2}$ miles
d After 10 miles

10 Choose any 3 digits and the decimal point from the cards on the right to make the nearest number you can to the ones listed. You can put the decimal point at the beginning, between the digits or at the end. One has already been done for you.

Nearest to 70 [6] [8] [·] [5]

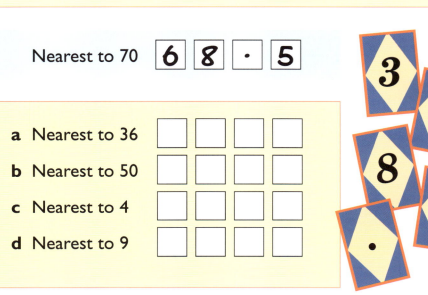

a Nearest to 36
b Nearest to 50
c Nearest to 4
d Nearest to 9

- as fractions
- adding
- subtracting

Percentages

Percentages are also a type of fraction. The symbol used is **%**. This stands for **per cent** which means **out of a hundred**.

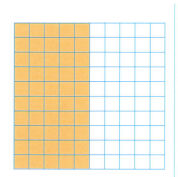

50% means **fifty out of a hundred** or $\frac{50}{100}$.

$\frac{50}{100}$ can be cancelled down. $\frac{50}{100} \div \frac{50}{50} = \frac{1}{2}$
So 50% is the same as $\frac{1}{2}$.

$25\% = \frac{25}{100}$
$\frac{25}{100} \div \frac{25}{25} = \frac{1}{4}$
So $25\% = \frac{1}{4}$

Changing percentages into fractions is easy if you remember that a percentage is really a number of hundredths and cancel the fraction down if possible.

1 Change these percentages to fractions, remembering to cancel down if possible.

a 30% = ☐   d 60% = ☐
b 10% = ☐   e 75% = ☐
c   5% = ☐   f   2% = ☐

By changing percentages into fractions, we can solve problems.

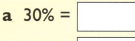

There should be 80 flights to Stella 5 this week. 25% are full. How many is that?

$25\% = \frac{25}{100} = \frac{1}{4}$
$\frac{1}{4}$ of the 80 flights are full.

20 flights are full.

2 Change percentages into fractions to answer these questions. Use a separate piece of paper for working out if necessary.

a The planet Stella 5 has 28 moons. 50% of them are blue in colour. How many are blue? ☐

b On Magna there are 160 life forms. 25% are human. How many humans are there? ☐

c 200 shuttles were serviced last month. 75% were damaged. How many was that? ☐

10% means $\frac{10}{100}$, which cancels down to $\frac{1}{10}$. To find $\frac{1}{10}$ of something, divide it by 10. The easiest way to do this is to move all the digits **one place** to the **right**.

	H	T	U	·		
10% of		9	0			
=			9			
10% of	£		5	·	0	0
=	£		0	·	5	0
10% of	£	2 4	7	·	0	0
=	£	2	4	·	7	0

3 What is 10% of each of these?

a £23·00

b 70 comets

c £5

d £12·50

e 2570 flights

f 90p

Once you know how to find 10%, finding 20%, 30%, 40% and so on is easy. 30% is simply 3 lots of 10%. 70% is 7 lots of 10%.

90 MULTOANS STRANDED IN SPACE! Only 30% rescued so far!

10% = $\frac{1}{10}$ $\frac{1}{10}$ of 90 Multoans = 9 Multoans

So 10% = 9 Multoans

30% (3 lots of 10%) = 3 × 9 = 27

30% of 90 Multoans = 27 Multoans

How many is that?

What is 1% of £8?

It is easy to find 1% of something if you remember that 1% is 1 hundredth ($\frac{1}{100}$). The easy way to divide by 100 is to **move the digits two places to the right**.

1% = $\frac{1}{100}$

$\frac{1}{100}$ of £8·00 = £0·08 (8p)

1% of £8 is 8p

4 Write down the answers to these problems. Use a separate piece of paper for your working.

a 1% of £7 =

b 20% of £8 =

c 1% of £15 =

d 30% of 500 =

e 90% of £60 =

f 1% of 8,500 =

If you can find 1%, finding 2%, 3%, 4% and so on is very easy. 2% is 2 lots of 1%. 7% is 7 lots of 1%.

$1\% = \frac{1}{100}$ $\frac{1}{100}$ of £12·00 = £0·12 (12p)

So 1% = 12p

7% (7 lots of 1%) = 7 × 12p = 84p

7% of £12 = 84p

5 Write the answers to these problems. Work them out on a separate piece of paper.

a 3% of £6 =

b 2% of £14 =

c 7% of £3 =

d 9% of £5 =

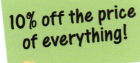

Sometimes we need to take away a percentage.

10% of £35 =
$\frac{1}{10}$ of £35 = £3.50

10% of £35 is £3.50

The Atlas was   £35·00
but take off   £ 3·50
and it now costs   £31·50

6 Write the new price of each of these items if they are reduced by 10%. Use a separate piece of paper for working out.

a Communicator £250

b Space socks £12

c Translator £11·50